Nelson's Last

Portsmouth, 14 Septen

Early in the morning of Saturday 14 September 1805, at about 6 a.m., a post chaise carrying Vice Admiral Lord Nelson passed through the Landport Gate on the north side of the massive fortifications ringing the town of Portsmouth. Swinging sharply to the left, along the foot of the ramparts, to the tree-fringed Townmount Bastion, it then turned right down the High Street. There, it drew up in front of the bow windows of The George Hotel and deposited its weary passenger, who had been on the road since 10.30 the previous evening.

Waiting in the hotel was Revd Henry Lancaster, the Rector of Merton in Surrey, where Nelson shared a house with his mistress, Emma Lady Hamilton. He had with him his young son who was joining Nelson's flagship, HMS *Victory*, as a midshipman. Leaving his son in Nelson's care, the Rector returned home, taking with him a note in Nelson's scrawling handwriting:

> My dearest and most beloved of women, Nelson's Emma. I arrived here this moment and Mr Lancaster takes this. His coach is at the door and waits only for my line. Victory is at St Helens and if possible shall be at sea this day. God protect you and my dear Horatia prays Ever Your Most faithful
>
> Nelson & Bronte[1]

After a quick breakfast, Nelson walked through the town, out of the Quay Gate overlooking the Camber, and across the Mill Dam to the Royal Dockyard, where he met with the Commissioner, Sir Charles Saxton. They discussed the ships that were being hurriedly fitted out to join the fleet that Nelson was to command, and he took the opportunity to issue a string of orders to their captains, couched in his trademark 'utmost urgency' style. After a summer of alarms, with fleet manoeuvres half across the world to the West Indies and back again, the combined fleets of France and Spain had been discovered in the Spanish port of Cadiz and Nelson was on his way out to deal with them once and for all. Seeking annihilation, he wanted to be sure that every available ship joined him as soon as possible. While in the Dockyard, he also took the opportunity to view the new Blockmills, where blocks for ships' rigging were being produced, using the country's first steam-powered production line.[2]

Returning to The George with Admiral Sir Isaac Coffin, an old friend, he found waiting for him two members of the Government who had come to wish him God-speed: George Rose, the Vice President of the Board of Trade, and the Treasurer to the Navy, George Canning. Another note went off to Emma, telling her, 'I have been overwhelmed with business from the moment of my arrival but you are never for one moment absent from my thoughts.' He also told her that Rose and Canning were going to join him on board the *Victory* to 'eat my scrambling dinner', a phrase that vividly conjures up the sense of urgent purpose he was exuding.[3]

He was now ready to board the *Victory*, which was waiting for him some three miles away at the anchorage at St Helen's, at the eastern end of the Isle of Wight. By now, word of his arrival had spread and a large crowd had gathered in the narrow street outside the hotel. The usual place of embarkation for officers was at the Sally Port, a large gate in the sea wall at the end of the High Street, just a few hundred yards away. But the crowd had grown so dense that it would have been extremely difficult for him to make his way through. So he decided to take an alternative route. Accompanied by Admiral Coffin, the two politicians, and by his two secretaries, Revd Alexander Scott and John Scott, he left The George by a back door giving onto a side street and began to head for the beach, where his barge had been ordered to meet him.

However, the crowd heard what he was doing and poured after him. Revd Thomas Socket, tutor to the sons of Lord Egremont, had brought his pupils over from Petworth to see Nelson depart and they got caught up in all the excitement:

> People crowded after him in all directions to get a sight of him. I was amused by the eagerness of a common sailor I met who was running with all his might and who, on being asked by another if he had seen him replied, 'No but d--n the old b---r I should like to see him once more', and posted away at top speed.[4]

Also in the crowd was an American, Benjamin Silliman who remembered, 'by the time he had arrived on the beach some hundreds of people had collected in his train, pressing all around and pushing to get a little before him to obtain a sight of his face.' Another account says that Nelson pressed his way through the mass of people good-humouredly, saying that he was sorry he did not have two arms so that he could shake hands with more friends.[6]

His route to the beach lay through a narrow tunnel in the ramparts, close to the King's Bastion, with its battery of guns commanding the approaches to Portsmouth Harbour. This led to a drawbridge over the moat connecting to an outlying work, the Spur Redoubt, from which another battery of guns covered the deep-water channel into Portsmouth. From the redoubt, a small door, or 'sally port', led out onto the beach, where Captain Thomas Hardy of the *Victory* was waiting with the Admiral's barge, close to the bathing machines.

As Nelson stepped onto the beach, the people following him began to crowd onto the ramparts overlooking his point of embarkation. The batteries were, of course, military establishments, guarded by sentries, who tried to stop the people gaining access to them, but they soon found themselves overwhelmed by sheer weight of numbers and helplessly wedged in the crowd. Among them was Benjamin Silliman, who later remembered:

> I stood on one of the batteries near where he passed and had a full view of his person. He was elegantly dressed and his blue coat splendidly illuminated with stars and ribbons. As the barge in which he embarked pushed away from the shore, the people gave three cheers which his Lordship returned by a waving his hat.'[7]

As he settled back into his seat in the stern of the barge, and as the well-trained crew picked up their stroke and began the long row to St Helen's, Nelson turned to Hardy and said, ' I had their huzzas before: I have their hearts now.'[8]

Reconstructing the Route

Even though it is such a well-known event, the exact route of Nelson's Last Walk has always proved difficult to establish, since no-one recorded it at the time. As a result, a number of misconceptions have arisen. The most famous depiction of his departure, by A. C. Gow, shows him descending the steps at the High Street Sally Port, which we know is wrong. Even the markers placed at various times in the area of the walk have been misleading. The Victorians erected one of the Victory's anchors close to the spot where he got into his boat but later, when the Clarence Parade funfair was constructed, it was moved - and in the wrong direction! It ended up some 350 yards away from where he actually embarked.[9]

'Farewell to Nelson', by A. C. Gow. Impeccable in its detail of costume and uniform, Gow's great romantic painting contains one major error - Nelson is shown leaving from the Sally Port in Old Portsmouth.

Nonetheless, as the account given above shows, modern research has enabled us to establish the route with rather more precision than hitherto. The starting point of the quest was Nelson's own words. He wrote in his private diary: 'At six o'clock arrived at Portsmouth and having arranged all my business, embarked at the Bathing Machines with Mr. Rose and Mr. Canning.'[10] He also wrote a note to his old friend Rear Admiral George Murray, in which he said, 'I am this moment getting in the Boat at the Bathing Machines.'[11]

3

It is known that the bathing machines were on the beach at Southsea, then just beginning to develop as a seaside resort. During research for the original edition of this monograph, a watercolour showing a view of the entrance of Portsmouth Harbour from Southsea Beach was located in the collection of the Portsmouth City Museum.[12] Although fairly crude and amateurish, it nevertheless shows the machines quite clearly on the beach, roughly where the large funfair now stands. This siting is confirmed by a later map, of about 1830, showing the bathing machines in a similar position.

Having established the approximate location of the spot where Nelson actually embarked, it was then possible to work back to discover how he reached it. In 1805, there was no direct route from the town of Portsmouth to Southsea - the King William Gate, which later gave access through the ramparts to the growing resort, was not constructed until 1833. Once again, the Portsmouth City Museum collections provided a clue: this time in the shape of plans of the fortifications.[13] These show that there was only one exit to the beach from the south eastern

The Spur Redoubt. Watercolour. Portsmouth City Museum, PCM 52/1952.

corner of Portsmouth town. Clearly marked 'Sally Port', it consisted of a tunnel leading from the Governor's Green through the ramparts to a drawbridge crossing the moat, to the Spur Redoubt, erected in 1680 to defend the seaward front of the defences. From the Redoubt itself, a small passage through the outer walls (also marked 'Sally Port') opened directly onto the beach, within about 150 yards of where the bathing machines were positioned. Clearly, therefore, this is most likely to have been the route that Nelson took.

This supposition was confirmed when Benjamin Silliman's account of Nelson's departure was first published in the United Kingdom by Allison Lockwood in 1985.[14] As we have already noted, Silliman mentions that he 'stood on one of the batteries' and watched Nelson get into his boat. He also makes it clear that he was close enough to see the details of his uniform, and to observe him waving his hat. The only battery overlooking the stretch of beach where Nelson embarked, and close enough for Silliman to make his detailed observations, is the King's Bastion. And the bastion directly overlooks the drawbridge leading to the Spur Redoubt.

Bathing machines on Southsea Beach. Watercolour. Portsmouth City Museums, PCM 79/1962.

So Silliman's eyewitness account supports the view that the tunnel through the ramparts, and the Sally Port in the Spur Redoubt, are most likely to have been the route taken by Nelson. This is further confirmed by Robert Southey's description of the scene in his 1813 biography of Nelson. He wrote of the people, 'pressing upon the parapet to gaze after him when his barge pushed off, and he was returning their cheers by waving his hat.'[15] For the crowd to be able see Nelson clearly, the point of embarkation must have been close to the ramparts - further confirmation that the 'Sally Port' route is the most likely one.

It is not possible to be so certain about the central part of Nelson's route. We know that he walked out of the back of The George into Penny Street and then down to where it joins Pembroke Road (then known as Green Row). But it is unclear whether he then cut straight across Governor's Green to reach the tunnel, or whether he walked along Green Row and then turned right, along the foot of the ramparts. Local tradition supports the longer, less direct route[16] but, so far, no documentary evidence has been found to support either possibility.

'Farewell my lads', by Fred Roe. Nelson in his barge, waving his hat as he is about to be rowed out to HMS Victory lying at St Helen's off the Isle of Wight.

Walking the Route

To tread in Nelson's footsteps (or fairly close to them), follow these directions:

1. Start in Penny Street, about 100 yards to the north of the junction with Pembroke Road. This is where the back door to The George Hotel was originally situated.

2. Turn left into Pembroke Road. The view across Governor's Green to the Garrison Chapel, and the ramparts beyond, is almost unchanged since Nelson's day - although the chapel lost the roof of its nave during the blitz in World War Two. Almost all the other buildings in the area are post-1805.

3. About 200 yards along Pembroke Street is a single storey redbrick building on the right hand side of the road. This is the old guard house for the King William Gate, erected in 1833. In 1805, the street terminated at this point, at the foot of the earth ramparts.

4. Immediately past the guard house, turn right down a narrow path along one side of Governor's Green. This could be the path Nelson took, with the earth ramparts towering above him on his left. However, as we have noted, it is also possible that Nelson walked directly across Governor's Green, in a south-heading diagonal from Penny Street to the King's Bastion.

5. At the end of the path, are the remains of the 18th century seaward defences, erected in 1730. The large mound on the left is the King's Bastion, from the top of which it is believed that Benjamin Silliman watched Nelson pass by. It is worth diverting at this point and walking up to the top of the bastion, from where there are stunning views out over Spithead, to the Isle of Wight. You will also be able to see clearly the route Nelson would have taken across the moat, and through the passage in the Spur Redoubt.

6. Returning to the foot of the bastion, find a low brick-lined arch, leading to a narrow, gravelled tunnel though the wall. This is the route it is now believed that Nelson took and so here it is likely you are treading directly in his footsteps.

7. The tunnel leads onto a bridge crossing the moat. Ahead are the foundations of the Spur Redoubt - the upper walls of the fortification were demolished to make way for the Esplanade.

8. Crossing the bridge, turn left into the Redoubt and walk a few yards along the path beside the moat, to where a narrow passage cuts through the redoubt wall. This is the 'Sally Port' through which Nelson passed and you can still see the iron hinges on which the heavy wooden doors were hung.

9. At this point, Nelson would have stepped straight onto the beach but it is no longer possible to do this. Instead, turn left, go up the metal steps to the car park and walk across to the sea wall. Alternatively, walk up the newly constructed ramp to the esplanade, and cross the wooden bridge that spans the foundations of the Spur Redoubt.

10. Once you are on the sea wall, you will be looking along the stretch of beach on which Nelson took his last land-based steps. The exact spot is now impossible to pinpoint but, in order for it to be within sight of the crowds on the King's Bastion, it must have been somewhere between the Spur Redoubt and the wall of the Clarence Parade funfair. If it is a clear day, you should be able to see the easternmost point of the Isle of Wight, St Helen's, where the *Victory* was waiting for her Admiral. If you turn back towards the land, and look up at the King's Bastion, you will perhaps be able to imagine the jostling crowd and hear the cheers ringing across the water as Nelson waves his hat in reply.

Author's Note

T his monograph was first published as an article in *The Nelson Dispatch*, the Journal of The Nelson Society, in July 1996. In view of the widespread interest it aroused, it was then reprinted as a pamphlet by the Society later that year. For this special bicentenary edition I have completely revised the text, and have taken the opportunity to introduce some new material, which has emerged in the intervening years. I have also altered the directions for following the route to incorporate the excellent new facilities recently introduced by Portsmouth City Council.

I should like to record my warm thanks to Derek Hayes, who edited the first edition and saw it through to publication and to Peter Clayton who has been responsible for this latest edition. I am also most grateful to my colleagues at the Portsmouth City Museum for their ready assistance in locating the local material on which my conclusions about Nelson's route are based and for assistance in supplying illustrations.

Colin White
Portsmouth, June 2005